SUCCESSFULLY LIVING THE CHRISTIAN LIFE

Written by

DR KINGSLEY OTURU
(MBBS, PHD)

DEDICATION

This Book is dedicated to my family

COPYRIGHT

Successfully Living the Christian Life

By

Kingsley Oturu

©Copyright K. Oturu 2022

The Publisher
Anointed Vibes (Voice of Thanksgiving) Publishers
For correspondence purposes contact: -

holyghostchapeluk@yahoo.com

www.holyghostchapel.org

All scripture quotations are from new American Standard or King James Bible except where otherwise stated.

Obtainable from online retail stores and Churches **globally.**

ACKNOWLEDGEMENTS

Firstly, I give thanks, honour and praise to the Almighty God through our Lord Jesus Christ who prodded me to write this book. I am particularly appreciative to the following people for their support encouragement and love: my loving son, Joshua Oturu, my wife, my parents (Bishop (Dr.) & Rev. (Mrs.) Mark Oturu), my fantastic brothers, Christopher, David, and Alexander, my loving sister, Victoria for her moral and spiritual support.

I must appreciate Bishop Francis and Pst Margaret Boampong (Intercessory Ministry of Great Britain). I am grateful to Pst Prophetess Eunice Simpson. Thanks also to Pst Kemi Adesola. I appreciate Sis. Lady Waynett Peters, Hon. (Princess) Peace Echeonwu, Andy Johnston, Laurence Jenkins, Prof Raphael and Doris Mrode, Chris and Debbie Ajala, African Carribean Christian Fellowship, Evang. Wole and Blessing Obawole, Emeka and Ifeoma Offor, IgboAmaka Edinburgh, Ariam Usaka Development Union, Leith Churches Together and Arthur Okongwu. I appreciate Bishop Oyedepo (Winners Chapel), Pastor Dele Bamgboye, High Flyers Church, Port Harcourt and every other person that has provided uplifting messages. God bless you mightily in the Mighty Name of Jesus Christ. Amen.

I appreciate My uncles and aunties (Adolphus Okebugwu, Ngozi Anyogu, Gabriel and Ngozi Azubuike) and brothers in the Lord who helped in seeing that this book is printed and are hereby acknowledged. I appreciate Chiamaka Anaedu, Prety Mutale, Stella Otuh and Ntachi Okuwa.

TABLE OF CONTENT

Chapter 1
Man's free will, God's grace and holiness

Man has always wanted to be independent from God. In the garden of Eden, God placed man within His Kingdom. The kingdom of God has been described by the theologian Wayne Grudem, as 'God's people (Adam and Eve) in God's place (the garden of Eden) under God's rule (you may eat from every tree in the garden apart from the tree of knowledge of good and evening)'. Man, often has a disdain for rules. People want to live without the constraints of rules. However, rules and principles help bring order in a complex world. Imagine if there were no motor rules. Cars could simply ignore the traffic rules and go through a red light. Imagine if there were no air traffic rules. Pilots can airlift and land as they please without regard of anything happening in the air. It may initially lead to less waiting times for passengers in airports. The result will be chaos and avoidable accidents. Even though God has given man rules to live by, He has also given man free will to choose. Free will may be defined as the putative ability of man to make choices as he pleases. God has given man a free will to choose if he will serve Him or not. This free will is given to man before salvation and continues even after man is saved. The saved man is not a robot and has the ability if he is willing, to obey God's commandment and serve Him in holiness through the power of the Holy Spirit. This issue is crucial in the way the evangelistic message of God's salvation through Jesus Christ is presented.

What is man that God is mindful of him?

Man is created in the image of God as a complicated being. Man is a spirit made in the image of God with a soul and lives in body[1]. Adam was created from the dust of the earth (Genesis 1:26-27). Another term that refers to the bodily nature of man is the term 'flesh' (Basar) as depicted in Isaiah 10:18 and John 1:14. Jesus says in Mark 12:30, *"you should love the lord your God with all your heart and with all your soul and with your entire mind and with all your strength"* [2]. The term 'strength' (Geber) denotes the bodily aspect of man (Exodus 10:11). The soul is the self-conscious life with

---

[1] Luehrmann, M *Lecture notes on doctrine of man.* Faith Mission Bible Institute Edinburgh 2009
[2] Grudem W *Systematic Theology* IVP 1994

feelings and desires. It includes man's will, intellect and emotions (Proverbs 20:27, 1Corinthians 14:14-15; 15:45, Hebrews 4:12 and Ephesians 4:23). It relates outwards to the social aspect of man. This is in contrast to the spirit (Ruach) that tends to communicate upwards towards the spiritual channel to God[3]. Man's spirit endows him with the capacity to commune with God in worship.

The term heart and spirit are often used interchangeably in scripture (John 4:24). The mind (Dianonia) is the part of man involved in intellectual activity. It is darkened in the natural man and unable to understand the things of God (1 Corinthians 2:14). The Holy Spirit relates with the spirit of man to convert the soul (Ephesians 2:3; 4:18). The Hebrew term for the heart is 'Lebab'. These immaterial parts are intertwined and interpenetrated with a very thin line dividing them as 'Lebab' includes not only the motives, feelings, affections, desires but also the will, principles and intellect of man.[4] (2 Samuel 7:3, 1 Chronicles 22:7). Man is a complex being with will and emotions.

---

[3] Purkiser W, Taylor R and Taylor W *God, Man and Salvation: A biblical theology.* Becon Hill Press 1977
[4] Pinnock, C. *The Grace of God, the will of man.* Zondervan Publishing House. 1989

The fall of man, free will and the human will

The human will of man was corrupted when man fell in the Garden of Eden (Genesis 2:16-17, 1 John 2:16, Romans 4:15; 5:12-14). The human will in the unsaved man is in contravention to the will of God (Jeremiah 17:9, Romans 8:7-8). However, the free will of man through the power of the Holy Ghost conviction, allows man to choose God's salvation and align his will to God's will (John 16:8).

Before 'the fall', man had the ability to choose if he would obey God's law not to eat the forbidden fruit or disobey and eat the fruit. The devil deceived Eve, who gave the fruit to Adam and he ate. They both chose to obey the devil and eat the forbidden fruit. This free will of man still persists after the fall of man. In Joshua 24:15, the children of Israel are not coerced to serve God. Instead, they are asked to choose who they will serve but advised to choose God as that will be more advantageous.

God is good and sovereign but yet chooses to allow man to have free will[5]. It is not God's will that restricts man's free will, but the fall and our sin nature that restricts our will from wanting and being able to choose God [6]. Man's free will is allowed within the sovereignty of God's will. It is not God's will that any man should perish but that all should be brought to repentance (1 Peter 3:9).

If the will of God, supersedes man's free will, then that would mean that no man will go to hell as it is not God's will for any to perish. This conclusion will be inaccurate however, as not everyone in the world is going to be saved. Only those who are born again of the water and of the Spirit and are in the lamb's book of life will be saved (John 3:16-20, Revelations 20:15). This places a responsibility on man to exercise his free will and give his life to Christ (John 3:16, Acts 16:31).

Although God has pre-selected or chosen men to be saved by His will and Grace, man still has to exercise his free will to be linked with God's will and be saved[7] (John 15:16, Isaiah 45:4). When man aligns his 'free will' to that of God's will, then God works within man to transform his 'human will' to do the will of God through the Holy Spirit. It is God that works in man

---

[5] Olson, R. *Arminian Theology: Myths and Realities* IVP Academic 2006
[6] Grudem, W. *Systematic Theology* IVP 1994
[7] Wynkoop, M. *Foundations of Wesleyan-Arminian Theology* Beacon Hill Press 1967

both to will and do of His good pleasure (Philippians 2:13). A proper understanding of the nature of man's will is crucial in the delivery of evangelistic messages.

In the UK someone may be 'preselected' for a credit card. The credit card is already theirs. However, the selected individual will not be forced to choose the credit card. They have free will to accept or reject the card. If they choose to accept the card, they will be provided with a card and credit limit of equity that they can draw from. In the same way, through the Blood of Jesus, mankind has been 'preselected' by God to be saved. However, man has to apply His free will and accept the gift of salvation from God to draw from the benefits of the Kingdom.

The nature of man, evangelism and salvation

Man is lost in sin. However, man is able to change and live a holy life that is needed to make heaven only through faith in Jesus Christ (2 Corinthians 5:17). The blood of Jesus shed on the cross, blots out the transgression of man and allows him free access to God[8] (Ephesians 2:13, Hebrews 10:19). Paul in Romans 5:2-5; 20-21 contends vigorously that the grace of God

---

[8] Oturu, K. *You can overcome by the blood of Jesus.* Anointed Vibes Publishers 2001

through the power of the Holy Spirit enables man with an imparted power to overcome sin[9]. Without holiness, no man can see the Lord (Hebrews 12:14). The Holy Spirit is able to make the sinner alive in Christ, be delivered from all sin and have relationship with God [10](Romans 9:28). A Christian who is led according to the Spirit has the ability to live in holiness (1 John 3:9; 5:18, Galatians 5:16). Apart from walking in holiness, the Christian filled with the power of the Holy Spirit is able to do miracles and cast out demons (Mark 16:17). This is because Jesus did all these and asserts that Christians will be able to do greater works than He did (John 14:12).

Man's free will remains intact and unrestricted before the fall, during and after salvation[11]. God in His sovereignty allows man to fall away if he chooses even after receiving the Holy Spirit (Hebrews 6:4-6, Hebrews 10:26). After redemption, man still has the choice to live in holiness in accordance with the empowerment of the Holy Spirit. As Romans 12:1 confirms, the saved

---

[9] Purkiser W, Taylor R and Taylor W *God, Man and salvation : A biblical theology.* Becon Hill Press 1977

[10] Dunning H *Grace , faith and holiness: A Wesleyan Systematic Theology.* Beacon Hill Press 1988

[11] Purkiser W, Taylor R and Taylor W. *God, Man and salvation: A biblical theology.* Becon Hill Press 1977

man is transformed by the renewing of the mind with the word of God. Christian spirits are transformed into the same image of God by the Spirit of the Lord (2 Corinthians 3:18; 5:17, 1 John 3:2-3). It is not the body that is transformed but the spirit of man.

The Spirit of God works by the word of God in the heart of man to renew his mind and transform his spirit and save his soul (James 1:21, Psalm 19:7). This leads to a transformation of the human will by the power of the Holy Ghost during conversion to follow the will of God[12] (Philippians 2:13). The decision to serve God leads to growth in spirituality and sensitivity to the Holy Spirit through studying the Word of God and prayers (Philippians 2:12, 1 Peter 2:2, Jude 1:20). In contrast, a decision to live in sin leads to hardening of the heart[13].

Under the cover of God's will, man's salvation is predicated on man's willingness to accept Jesus as Lord and Saviour. "Whosoever wills, let him take the water of life freely." (Revelation 22:17). Our spirits are saved at salvation. Our souls are being saved as we engage

---

[12] Oturu, K. *The Holy Ghost Revelation*. Omki Publishers 1995

[13] Wynkoop, M *Foundations of Wesleyan-Arminian Theology* Beacon Hill Press 1967

with the Word of God. Our bodies will be fully redeemed at the second coming of Christ.

References/Bibliography

1) Dunning, H. *Grace , Faith and Holiness: A Wesleyan Systematic Theology.* Beacon Hill Press 1988

2) Grudem, W. *Systematic Theology* IVP 1994

3) Luehrmann, M. *Lecture Notes on Doctrine Of Man.* Faith Mission Bible Institute Edinburgh 2009

4) Oturu, K. *The Holy Ghost Revelation.* Omki Publishers 1995

5) Oturu, K. *You Can Overcome by The Blood of Jesus.* Omki Publishers 2001

6) Pinnock, C. *The Grace of God, The Will of Man.* Zondervan Publishing House. 1989

7) Purkiser W, Taylor, R and Taylor, W. God, *Man and salvation : A biblical theology.* Becon Hill Press 1977

8) Wilson, R . *Arminian Theology: Myths and Realities* IVP Academic 2006

9) 9)Wynkoop, M. *Foundations of Wesleyan-Arminian Theology* Beacon Hill Press 1967

Chapter 2
Jesus Christ: Fully God and fully man

Introduction

Jesus Christ is described in the Bible as the Son of God (John 1:34,39) and as the Son of Man (Matthew 8:20). These titles point to the divine and humanistic natures of the one person of Christ respectively. However, in analysing the person of Christ there is the danger of misinterpreting the relationship of His two natures. Although the dual nature of Christ is a mystery that requires Godly revelation to understand, Jesus is both fully God and fully man. Jesus Christ's human nature is hardly debatable against the background of scriptural and historical evidence as to His earthly existence. This chapter is organised in 3 sections.

In the first section, the divine nature of Jesus is expounded. In the second section, the human nature of Jesus is explored. In the last section, the importance of

Jesus being fully divine and being fully human is linked to the life of the Christian.

Dual nature of Jesus Christ: A look at Chalcedon

Following a series of discussions about the person of Christ among different Church councils (council of Nicaea, Constantinople, Ephesus), this culminated in a council meeting called by emperor Marcian in 451 A.D. with 630 bishops in attendance. This was the council of Chalcedon. The summary of their deliberation is that Jesus is truly human, truly divine united in One Person with the two natures being inseparably united, and yet not mingled or confounded. As Berkouwer G argues, Chalcedon is not an explanation of the dual nature of Christ[14]. Rather, it is a proclamation of faith based on scripture. I agree with the argument that in trying to explain rather than accept the mystery of God, there is danger of falling into one of the Christological heresies (Separating Christ's nature- Nestorianism, mixing them into one nature –Eutychianism , denying His human nature- Apolliniaranism or denying His divine

---

[14] Berkouwer G *Studies In Dogmatics: The Person of Christ.* Eedmans Publishing company, 1977

nature- Arianism)[15]. The mystery is that the Son of God took on the form of human flesh to die for man and link man back to God. In understanding this mystery, it is imperative not to stop at Chalcedon but to look at scripture (the Word) to understand the nature of Christ. In the beginning was the Word and the Word was with God and the Word was God (John 1:1). It is only in the Word that we can gain some understanding of the mystery of Jesus being God and Man.

Jesus' confirmation of His divine nature

Jesus gives witness of His oneness with God when he said in John 10:30 that He and the Father are one. This means that they are of the same essence. Although the Person of the Father and Jesus the Son are the different, they are one God. The divine nature of Jesus Chris is also implied in His pre-existence. Jesus also declares in John 8:58, 'before Abraham was, I AM'. I AM THAT I AM is the name reserved only for God. Jesus also confirms in John 6:33 that He came to world from heaven in order to give life.

---

[15] Grudem W *Systematic Theology: An introduction to Biblical doctrine.* Inter-varsity Press, 1994

Fatherly confirmation of Jesus Christ's Divine nature.

The Sonly nature of Christ is also pointed out by God the Father during Christ's baptism and on the mount of transfiguration (Matthew 3:17; Matthew 17:5). God the Father attests that Jesus is His beloved Son, in which He is well pleased. Even the Jews sought to kill Him because He called God His Father, thus making Himself equal to God (John 5:17-19). The title 'Son of God' points to the deity of Christ and His relationship to God the Father[16]. The divine nature of Jesus Christ suggests that those worship and honour Him also worship God. All may honour the Son as they honour the Father and those who don't honour the Son, do not honour the Father that sent Him (John 5:21-23).

Apostolic affirmation of Christ's Divinity

There are apostolic confirmations of the Godly nature of Christ. Peter admits that Jesus is the Son of God (Matthew 16:16) while Thomas exclaims that Jesus is his lord and his God (John 20:28). In a similar vein, Paul praises Jesus Christ as God blessed forever

____

[16] Grogan G *The Christ of the Bible and the Church's faith.* Christian Focus Publication, 1998

(Romans 9:5). He also prophesies of the appearing of the glory of the 'Great God and our Saviour Jesus Christ' in the last days (Titus 2:13). The Hebrew writer refers to Jesus Christ being the express image of God.

Peter attests that the Spirit of Christ was within the prophets of the Old Testament revealing Himself to them (1Peter 1;10-12). Examples are seen in Isaiah 9:6, where the Prophet Isaiah describes Jesus as Immanuel and mighty God and in Zechariah 6:12-13, where the Kingly and Priestly nature of Jesus is prophesied. John affirms that all things were made through Him and without Him was anything made that was made. This is also corroborated in 1 Corinthians 8:6 and Colossians 1:16.

The Hebrew writer also confirms that through Him, God created the world (Hebrews1:2). God created the world through His word. However, the word was not simply a sound but a person. That person is Jesus Christ who holds together the whole world and universe (Colosians 1:17; Hebrews 1;3). Without Jesus, the orderliness of the world will be thrown into confusion. As John Brand and Geoffrey Grogan argue, scientific discoveries simply authenticate the consistent nature of God in upholding the universe by the word of His power[17] [18]. Jesus has always been with God from the beginning and is God.

Scripture pointing to the manly nature of Christ

Apart from being God, Jesus is also a man. Jesus described Himself as a man who tells the truth (John8:40). The human dimension of Christ nature is evident when He describes Himself as the Son of man (Matthew 8:20; Mark 2:10; Luke 5:24). This title denotes His earthly relationship with man and His dominion on earth. While on earth, Jesus could get tired (John 4:6). He had a soul that was troubled before His crucifixion (John 12:27).

Before His crucifixion, Pontius Pilate also exclaimed 'Behold the man!' (John 19: 5). Jesus had a plethora of human emotions. He groaned in His spirit and was troubled (John 11:33). He wept (John 11:35). He loves (John 14:21). He was dependent of God the Father as evidence by His praying to Him (Luke 22:44). He admits that the Father is greater than Him (John 14:28). He

---

[17] Brand J *Lecture on the providence of God*. Faith Mission Bible Institute. Edinburgh, 2009

[18] Grogan G *I want to know what the Bible says about Jesus.* Kingsway publications Sussex, 1977

needed angelic strengthening in the garden of Gethsemane (Luke 22:43). When asked about when the end of the world would come, He suggested that only the Father knows (Mark 13:32). Hence, in the form of man, He willingly limited His divine powers. Despite His manly nature, He was able to do some supernatural things by the power of God.

He however needed empowerment through the Holy Spirit. He was able to do miracles and taught the Word of God with authority so that it baffled the scribes and Pharisees (John 7:45). Jesus is also different from other men in that He is without sin (John 13:46; Hebrews 4:15).

Secular sources about the manly nature of Christ abound in the Tacitus (Annals 15, 444), Suetonius (life of Calaudius and life of Nero). Jewish sources such as Josephus (antiquities of the Jews) speak of James as the brother of Jesus the so-called Christ condemned to death of a cross by Pilate. The Talmud also refers to Jesus of Nazareth being crucified on the eve of Passover (Tractate Sanhedrin 43a)[19].

---

[19] Rogers S. *Lecture notes on doctrine of Christ: His unique person*. Faith Mission Bible Institute, 2009

The existence of Christ as man on earth is hardly debatable with these evidences. Christ needed to come to earth as man to sympathies with man and understand him.

The dualistic nature of Christ and the Christian

Christianity is different from other religions as God is seen not just as a distant being with little or no relation to man. He is seen as a father who cares for His Children just like an earthly father would normally care for and provide for his children (Deuteronomy 1:31). Through faith in Jesus Christ, gentiles and unbelievers can partake of this fatherly relationship with God through the Holy Spirit (John 8:58; Romans 8:1-31). Although Jesus has the same nature as God the Father, He is different from the person of God the Father. Jesus is not two persons. He is one person with two natures.

The two natures are inextricably linked. Before the incarnation, Jesus existed as God. He however, emptied Himself of His glory to come down to earth to save man. He returned back to His glory at the resurrection (John 3:13; John 17:5; Philippians 2:7).

In order for man to be redeemed back to God, there needed to be a mediator. That mediator is Jesus Christ.

Paul affirms that even though He was equal with God, He counted equality not something to be grasped but He humbled Himself, taking the form of a man (Philippians 2:17). Through the process of incarnation, the Word (Jesus) became flesh and dwelt among men; thus, becoming God and Man simultaneously (John 1:14). Jesus had to do this to understand man and link man back to God. Paul suggests that there is one man that links God back to man, the man Jesus Christ (1Timothy 2:5-6). Jesus also needed to come to earth to show man the way to walk in the fear of God. He died for mankind and was resurrected by the Holy Spirit (Romans 1:4; Colossians 1:18). With Jesus' resurrection and ascension back to heaven, He opened the way for the Holy Spirit to live in the life of all flesh and quicken man's mortal body on the last day of judgement (Romans 8:11). As Paul argues, if Jesus was not raised up from the dead, then the whole Christian faith is in vain (1 Corinthians 15:17). Before incarnation, Jesus only had the divine nature. The manly nature was acquired following the virgin birth. With the dual nature, Jesus is able to act as a High Priest to man as demonstrated in John 17:5. It was also the Father's good pleasure for Jesus to be made the pure sacrifice to wash man's sins, deliver man from the grip of the devil and make peace with God (Colossians 1:19-20).

This priestly nature continues perpetually until the day of judgement. He lives to continuously make intercession for the saints according to the will of God (Hebrews 7:25). Because He came as a man, he can sympathize with the infirmities of those who are tempted (Hebrews 2:18). Because He is God, He can intercede and mediate between man and God. Jesus the Son of God being infinite God and finite man in one person is a divine miracle and mystery that only the Holy Spirit can open the human mind to understand.

The cross: God's Cure for sin

A Christian's sin can be forgiven by the blood of Jesus (1 John 1:19). Similarly, the sins of unbelievers can be forgiven when they become born again by the blood of Jesus (John 3:16, Ephesians 1:7). However, Jesus warns about an unpardonable sin that can never be forgiven. This sin is to blaspheme against the Holy Spirit. In this essay, I argue that the blasphemy against the Holy Spirit is to speak irreverently against the Holy Spirit and to suggest that the Holy Spirit is an evil spirit.

Blasphemy against the Holy Spirit

In Matthew 12:22-32, Jesus healed a man who was demon possessed. The man was blind and dumb as a result of the demon possession. Jesus cast the demon out and healed the man by the power of the Holy Spirit. However, the Pharisees suggested that he cast out the demons by Beelzebub (the ruler of demons). Jesus then said that "any sin or blasphemy shall be forgiven but that blasphemy against the Spirit shall not be forgiven" (Matthew 12:31). Thus, he pronounced the fact that there is an unpardonable sin that can never be forgiven. However, there are many interpretations of what the sin is.

There have been some suggestions that the unpardonable sin refers to something that could only happen in Jesus' life time, the sin of unbelief in Jesus Christ, or a falling away of Christians in form of apostasy[20]. However, Jesus expatiates on what it means when He says that "he that speaks against the Holy Spirit shall never be forgiven" (Matthew 12:32). To blaspheme against the Holy Spirit means to speak irreverently or injuriously against Him. The Pharisees suggested that the Holy Spirit was actually an evil spirit

---

[20] Grudem, W "Systematic Theology" .Intervarsity Press, 1994

(Beelzebub). They were suggesting that Jesus could not have cast the demon by the Spirit of God but rather by an evil spirit.

To give glory to the devil for the work done by God is a great evil. God is a jealous God (Deuteronomy 6:15). He will not share His glory with anyone (Isaiah 42:8). To blaspheme is to willfully abuse the Holy Spirit or attribute the Spirit's work to the devil[21].   The unpardonable sin is not a sin that is done unconsciously or my mistake. It is a conscious, malicious and willful slander against the works and conviction of the Holy Spirit in Christ Jesus. Instead there is an attribution it out of hatred to the devil[22].

The warning of Christ for man not to blaspheme against the Holy Spirit, points to the fact that man should be not be quick to judge other ministers or men of God (Matthew 7:1-6). If a Christian is zealously doing the work of God by the Holy Spirit and someone suggests that He is doing the work by an evil spirit, the person is in danger of committing the unpardonable sin. An understanding that such a sin exists should

---

21 Parker, F Lecture notes on doctrine of sin, 2010
22 Berkhof , L *Systematic Theology* Banner of Truth 1996

enable Christians to live in fear of God and give glory to God.

References/Bibliography

1. Berkouwer, G *Studies In Dogmatics: The Person of Christ* Eerdmans Publishing company, 1977

2. Brand, J *Lecture on the providence of God.* Faith Mission Bible Institute, 2009

3. Grogan, G *I want to know what the Bible says about Jesus.* Kingsway publications Sussex, 1977

4. Grogan, G *The Christ of the Bible and the Church's faith.* Christian Focus Publication, 1998

5. Rogers, S *Lecture notes on doctrine of Christ: His unique person.* Faith Mission Bible Institute, 2009

6. Scroggie, W *A guide to the gospels.* Pickering and Inglis publishing ltd: London, 1973

7. Grudem W *Systematic Theology: An introduction to Biblical doctrine.* Inter-varsity Press. London, 1998

Chapter 3
The Holy Spirit in the Old Testament: present and active but not yet fully revealed

The Holy Spirit is the third person of the God head (2 Corinthians 3:17-18, Acts 5:3-4). Understanding His role in the Old Testament could help us apply lessons learnt in our lives. Before the incarnation and Pentecost, the Holy Spirit was involved in creation, inspiration empowerment and renewal. However, the Holy Spirit was not fully revealed.

This chapter is organised in 3 sections. In the first section, the person of the Holy Spirit is explored. In the second section the roles of the Holy Spirit in the Old Testament is expounded. In the last section, the limitations to the manifestation of the Holy Spirit is explored and linked to the personal experience of Holy Spirit that Christians can partake in following the death and resurrection of Jesus Christ.

Names of the Holy Spirit in the Bible

In theology, the law of first mention suggests that the first time a word is mentioned in the Bible contains deep truths and the original intention of that word. The first mention of the Holy Spirit is in Genesis 1:2-3. The power of the Holy Spirit was needed before the creative power of God could be perfected on earth. A similar move of the Holy Spirit is needed in the life of the Christian.

The Holy Spirit is depicted by many names in the Bible. These include, Holy Spirit, Spirit of God, Spirit of the LORD, Spirit of Christ, Holy Ghost and Spirit (Isaiah 63:10, Judges 6:34, Romans 8:9, Acts 10:47, Numbers 11:25). He is also depicted as the Breath of the almighty in Job 32:8. The same word for breath and spirit in the Hebrew text is 'Ruach'[23].

However, The Holy Spirit is not just a force. He is a person who can be grieved (Ephesians 4:20). In Isaiah 51:11, David asks God not to take His Holy Spirit from him. This plea suggests a form of peace, joy and fulfilment that David derived from communion with the Spirit. Notwithstanding, references to the Spirit in

---

[23] Roger, A Lecture notes on Doctrine of the Holy Ghost ,2010

the Old Testament tend to focus on the 'impersonal' dimensions of the Holy Spirit. These include the creative, inspiration, empowering and renewal powers of the Holy Spirit.

Activities of the Holy Spirit in the Old Testament

Creative power of the Spirit: The Holy Spirit was active in the creation of the world. He was also crucial in the creation of man. When God breathed his Spirit (breath) into Adam, he became a living Soul (Genesis 1:2). Psalm 104:30 also reveals that God created animals by His Spirit. The creative power of the Spirit of God in the birth of Jesus Christ is demonstrated just before incarnation in Luke 1:35. As the Spirit of God came upon Mary and the power of the Almighty overshadowed her, this resulted in the birth of Jesus Christ.

Inspiration of Scripture, prophecy and ecstatic experience

All scripture is inspired by God as holy men were moved by the Holy Spirit (2 Tim 3:16, 2 Peter 1:21). This means that every word in the Bible is God breathed. It is God's word for us today as when it was written. Hebrews 1:1-2 suggests further that the word of God was spoken through inspired prophets. The Spirit of God was involved in inspiring prophets of God to see visions and prophesy (Numbers 11:25, Ezekiel 2:2).

Empowerment of the Holy Spirit

The Holy Spirit also empowers people to do tasks they could not ordinarily do on their own. The Spirit of God empowered some sanctified servants of God like Bezalel to build the tabernacle of God (Exodus 31:3-5). The Spirit empowered the Judges of Israel with strength to rule Israel (Judges 3:10; 3:10; 14:6). Kings such as David were empowered by the Spirit with strength and skills to lead the children of Israel (1 Samuel 16:13). The prophets in the Old Testament were also empowered with wisdom, understanding and intellectual ability to solve critical problems (Daniel 4:8, Job 21:8)

Renewing power of the Holy Spirit

References are made in the Book of Isaiah and Ezekiel about the renewing power of the Holy Spirit (Isaiah 32:15, Ezekiel 36:27). The Spirit brings life and renewal. He gives a new heart to long for the things of

God. However, the readings appear to be prophetic of what was to come when the Spirit falls on those people who give their lives to Christ and enter the Kingdom of God.

The Spirit: Given to a few, temporarily for specific purpose

Although the Holy Spirit was present in the Old Testament, there is a sense that He was not fully revealed. As Billy Graham argues, the Holy Spirit in the Old Testament tends to rest on a selected type of persons for specific purposes[24].

These include prophets, Judges, kings and workers in the house of God. There is no way to predict who the Holy Spirit falls upon. Even when people were not walking according to the will of God, He still allowed His Spirit to fall upon them (1 Samuel 19:24). Hence, we cannot put God in a box. He fills who he wants to fill at his own time and at his own choosing. In the Old

____

[24] Graham, B "The Holy Spirit" London: Collins, 1979

Testament, the Spirit tends to leave the person after achieving the specific purpose for which He was sent.

The Holy Spirit in the Old Testament could not also baptise people into the Kingdom of God. Hence, the smallest in the Kingdom of God is greater than John the Baptist (Matthew 11:11). Through accepting Jesus as Lord and saviour, the Christian can be baptised through one Spirit into the kingdom of Christ (Matthew 3:11-12; 1 Corinthians 12:13).

Creation of a new heart but Holy Ghost power still needed

A more personal relationship with the Spirit is given to the Christian in the New Testament. There is a fruitful transformation as the Christian's heart is transformed (2 Corinthians 5:17). While in the Old Testament era, the Spirit was only available to special ones such as kings and prophets, Jesus' death and resurrection has opened the door for all believers to partake of the Spirit.

The Spirit is now available to guide and lead Christians on a permanent basis. In the Old Testament is there is also no mention of the gift of speaking in tongues which allows the spirit of the believer to pray as empowered by the Holy Spirit (Acts 2:4). God's master plan has always been to have a meaningful relationship with man through His Spirit. Through this relationship there should be a change in the heart of man and manifestation of the fruit, signs and wonders of God (Ezekiel 36:26).

However, it is important to note the activities of the Holy Spirit in the Old Testament are still relevant in the lives of Christians today. God is the same yesterday, today and forever. As Christians, we are to demonstrate the creative, inspirational, empowering and renewing power in our lives. It is important that Christians earnestly thirst and ask for the filling and refilling of the Holy Spirit so that we can move in the power of God and deliver people from the bondage of the kingdom of darkness.

Bibliography

1) Bruner, F "A Theology of the Holy Spirit" London: Hodder and Stoughton, 1970
2) Ferguson, S "The Holy Spirit – Contours of Christian Theology" Leicester: IVP, 1996
3) Graham, B "The Holy Spirit" London: Collins, 1979

Chapter 4
The names of God in the life of the Christian

God is Spirit. He has relational (or communicable) and essential (or incommunicable) attributes. The relational attributes relate to those attributes that God shares with man in a limited manner. They also point to ways in which God relates with man. Essential attributes are those characteristics of God that God alone shares. For example, God is infinite and everlasting[25]. It is difficult to grasp the essence of God with limitations of the human mind[26]. However, scripture provides us with some insight of His different attributes through His names. An analysis of the different names of God as contained in the Bible is undertaken with expatiation of His different attributes that they point to. The names of God are important. They reveal God's attributes. An understanding of the

------

[25] Grudem, W *"Systematic Theology"* Intervarsity Press 1994

[26] Reymond, R *'What is God?'* Christian Focus 2007

name of God and how it links to Christ, is crucial for living the Christian life successfully.

The importance of names

Names are very important. As Walter Dolen argues, names point to characteristics embodied in the person that possessed that name. People live out their names[27]. When Jabez was born, he was born in sorrow and given the name Jabez. Consequently, he lived a life of sorrow and pain. God had to intervene to enlarge Jabez's coasts (1 Chronicles 4:10). Similarly, Jacob (which means supplanter) lived the life of a fraudster. Jacob's name was changed to Israel (ruling with God) in Genesis 32:28 while Abram's (exalted father) name was changed to Abraham (father of many nations) in Genesis 17:5 for them to fulfil their God given destinies. These examples depict the importance of names.

In the Bible, God is addressed by different names. These names give us a glimpse, indication or insight as to his attributes. God's names and His attributes are intertwined. We know God's attributes through His names. An understanding of the different names of

---

[27] Walter, D *The God papers*. Becoming one Church press

God is important for a Christian to have the fear and reverence of him on the one hand, (based on his essential attributes) and love him based on his relational attributes on the other.

Essential names of God

Elohim (El): This is the first name of God recorded in the Bible in Genesis 1:1-2[28]. The name represents the omnipresence of God and is used when in an atmosphere of worship. The name encompasses the energy of God and has elements of fear and reverence. El is the singular form while Elohim is plural.

El shaddai: points to the fact that God is the all sufficient one. It points to the fact that God is more than enough for the Christian. If the Christian needs a miracle, healing, protection, financial breakthrough or any other need, God is enough. The name is first used by Abraham in Genesis 17:8, when God supernaturally provides a ram in replace of Isaac for sacrifice.

El Elyon: means that God is Most High. In Genesis 14:17-20 and numbers 24:16, Elyon is used in form of worship to recognise the highness of God in relation to

---

[28] Roger, S *Lecture notes on Doctrine of God* Edinburgh, 2009

his creation. He is higher than any other created being. He is higher than any problem. He is higher than demonic forces.

El Olam: points to the everlasting attribute of God. God exists in time and acts on time[29]. He has no end. He is everlasting and unchangeable (Genesis 21:33; Psalm 102:25-27). An understanding of this, allows the Christian not to focus on the limited life on earth, but the everlasting destiny of joy that is contained in God.

El Roi: points to the fact that God sees all. He saw Haggai in Genesis 16:13 when she was in difficulty and brought help in form of a well. God sees His children and will always cause all things to work together for good (Romans 8:20-26). The eyes of the Lord run through the whole earth to fight for those whose hearts are perfect towards Him (2 Chronicles 16:9). He never sleeps nor slumbers. He is faithful. The names above depict incommunicable attributes of God which created beings do not possess.

---

[29] Grudem, W *"Systematic Theology"* Intervarsity Press 2007

The Lordship of God

God loves man and wants to rule over and with him. **Adonai** name of God points to the fact that God is our master and Lord who needs to be obeyed. It is a substitute for Jehovah thought too holy to even be pronounced. The name is used in Isaiah 6:1-6. In order to win man back to Himself, He had to send His Son Jesus to bring about a change in man's heart and redeem man back to Himself (John 3:16). He chooses to have relations with man through covenants.

Covenant name of God

The covenant name of God is YHWH, Yahweh or Jehovah (Genesis 2:4). This name is depicted as LORD in the Bible. It refers to the absolute independence and self-existence of God. The meaning of the name is revealed to Moses in Exodus 3:13-15, where God refers to Himself as 'I AM THAT I AM'. The name is a mystery and may point to the fact that in God, the past, presence and future is combined. According to the International Standard Bible encyclopedia, it should actually be translated 'I WILL BE THAT I WILL BE' from the original Hebrew text[30]. In other words, God is whatever He wills to be to His children. To those who need protection, He is their protection. To those who need salvation, He is salvation. He will be that He will be. These are expatiated in the relational names of God. Jehovah is a covenant name that shows that God will fight on behalf of His children (Psalms 83:19), be a rock of protection and stability (Exodus 15:3) and is an unchanging God who will ensure that His children are not consumed by the enemy (Malachi 3:6). Other branches of the covenant names of God are hereby highlighted in the relational names of God.

Relational names of God

The relational names of God are compound names of Jehovah that show how God relates to His children and correspond to redemptive experiences of God. **Jehovah-Tsidkenu,** highlights the fact that God is righteous (Jeremiah 23:6), while **Jehovah M'qaddishkem** points to the fact that God is Holy (Exodus 31:13). The righteousness of God denotes the fact that God is right in His judgements and decisions. Holiness of God points to the awesomeness of God

---

[30] Dolen, W *What is God's name.* 2003 Available on line at
http://becomingone.org/gp/gp1b.htm

because He is pure, separate from man and sinless (2 Corinthians. 5:21). An understanding of the righteousness and Holiness of God should cause the Christian to come before Him in fear and reverence (Leviticus 20:7, 8).

Jehovah Jireh, shows that God is the one who provides (Genesis22:8). He will supply all our needs according to His riches in glory (Philippians 4:19). An understanding of God's provision capacity will allow a Christian to live without stress and anxiety as he/she is rest assured that God is the good provider.

Jehovah Shalom, is a God of peace. He will keep those in perfect peace whose minds are stayed on Him (Isaiah. 26:3). God is peace (Judges 6:14). Peace is not found in alcohol, drugs or through socialisation. Only God can give real peace in a time of uncertainty and unreliability in the world.

Jehovah Nissi points to the fact that God is a banner for His children to shield them from every evil arrow or wiles of darkness (Psalm 60:4). The protective power in the name of God is evident in the life of the Christian. God is referred to as **Jehovah Sabaoth** (the Lord of hosts) who is a fortress (Psalm 46:7). The fortress is a place of protection. Proverbs 18:10 allows us to understand that the name of the Lord is a strong tower. The righteous run into it and are saved.

Jehovah Rapha shows that the Lord is a healer. He heals emotionally and physically of all sicknesses and diseases. God suspends natural laws for His own pleasure to show Himself strong through miracles and healings (Exodus 15:26; Psalm 107:20).

Jehovah Rohi, is a shepherd who guides His children (Psalm 23:1; Genesis 48:15). In the Old Testament and currently, God guides His children through His word and through His Holy Spirit. The power in the word of God is immense. As powerful as God's name is, God has exalted His word above all His names (Psalm 138:2).

Jehovah-Sharnma is God who is there (Ezekiel 48:35). This name points to the omnipresence of God. God is everywhere including Heaven and Hades (Psalm 139:8). In every situation, God is there. Since, God is there, the Christian can be rest assured that he will cause everything to work together for good and His will and purpose (Eph. 1:11).

The name of Father

Christianity is different from other religions as God is seen not just as a distant being with little or no relation to man. He is seen as a father of the nation of Israel (Hosea 11:1). He cares for His Children just like an earthly father would normally care for and provide for his children (Deuteronomy 1:31). Through faith in Jesus Christ, gentiles and unbelievers can partake of this fatherly relationship with God through the Holy Spirit (John 8:58; Romans 8:1-31).

The names of God are embodied in the name of Jesus

Exploring the names of God is not simply some distant theological expository exercise that has no relevance in the life of a Christian. I hereby argue that the names of God are all embodied now in the name of Jesus. The names of God also relate to the Christian in the here and now. When Jesus died on the Cross of Calvary and rose again, He provided a link to bring fallen man back to God. Jesus, who is also God, has been given a name that is above every other name (Philippians 2:9). Hence El Elyon (The Most-High God) is embodied in the name of Jesus. At the name of Jesus, every knee shall bow in heaven and on earth.

As the prophets in scripture prophesy, all nations will be brought back to honour God in the name of the LORD (Zephaniah 3:9; Jeremiah 3:17). The name of the Father, the Son and the Holy Spirit are all one name (Matthew 28:19).

Paradoxically, in the name of Jesus is the name of God and in the Name of God is the name of Jesus because God has given His name to Jesus (John 17:11-12). Jesus is the Greek translation of the name Joshua. The original Hebrew name of Jesus is Joshua[31]. Etymologically, Joshua is a combination of two elements[32]. These are YHWH (which is the name of the LORD) and Yeshua (which means salvation). If the two elements are put together, Jesus is actually means JEHOVAH (LORD) who SAVES. Jehovah who saves (Jesus) is the name of God that is above every other name. In Jesus there is healing, protection, provision, peace and all the other relational attributes of God. If

---

[31] Dolen W *What is God's name.* Available on line at http://becomingone.org/gp/gp1b.htm. Accessed on 8/1/11

[32] Meaning and Etymology of the name Joshua. Available on line at http://www.abarim-publications.com/Meaning/Joshua.html. Accessed on 8/1/2011

the Christian asks any of these things from God, in Jesus' name, they will be provided.

In conclusion, the names of God point to the awesomeness and holiness of God on the one hand, and the relations with His children on the other. These names are now embodied in the name of Jesus. The Christian needs to recognise and understand these names to fear and reverence God and partake in the covenant promises of God.

References/Bibliography

1) Dolen, W *The God papers*. Becoming one Church press 2003
2) Dolen, W *What is God's name*. Available on line at http://becomingone.org/gp/gp1b.htm. Accessed on 8/1/2011
3) Reymond, R 'What is God?' Christian Focus 2007
4) Roger, S *Lecture notes on Doctrine of God* Edinburgh, 2009
5) Grudem, W "Systematic Theology" Intervarsity Press 1994
6) Uittenbogaard, A *Meaning and Etymology of the name Joshua*. Available on line at http://www.abarim-publications.com/Meaning/Joshua.html. Accessed on 8/1/2011

Chapter 5
Should Christians go to Church?

The church is the gathering of God's people under Christ's headship who come together in accordance with Christ's prescription for the purpose of collective worship, testimony, administration of ordinances, mutual edification and exercise of government and discipline[33].

The church is comprised of an invisible and visible component. Christians need not only to be part of the invisible church but also actively participate in the activities of the visible local church. It is through participation in worship and service in the visible church that the Christian ultimately partakes in the fellowship of the invisible church.

The invisible and visible church

---

[33] Luehrmann, M *Lecture notes Church doctrine.* Faith Mission Bible Institute Edinburgh 2009

The invisible church is the church as God sees it[34]. It comprises of the many Christians which may belong to one of many church denominations around the world[35]. Only those who have given their lives to Christ are part of the invisible church (Matthew 7:21-24, 1 Samuel 16:7).

However, it is not sufficient for a Christian to say he/she is a member of the invisible church and not participate in the local church[36].

The visible church is the physical manifestation of the spiritual church observable by the community. The church is the body of Christ as each member of the church is a living stone in the building of Christ (1 Peter 2:5). The church is both an institution and observable living organism through which God can manifest His glory to the world by His Spirit (Ephesians 4:4-6, Ephesians 2:19-22).

Reasons for being active in the church

[34] Grudem, W *"Systematic Theology"* Intervarsity Press 1994
[35] Luehrmann, M *Lecture notes Church doctrine.* Faith Mission Bible Institute Edinburgh 2009
[36] Harris, J *Stop Dating The Church: Fall in love with the family of God,* Moltnoma Publishers 2004

To obey God

God commands Christians not to forsake the gathering of the saints (Heb. 10:24-26). Coming to church is not a leisurely activity to be done at our spare time. It is a commandment from God to ensure that Christians encourage each other in the Lord[37]. It is also in an atmosphere of church worship that the ordinances of God such as the Holy Communion and baptism can be obeyed[38] (Acts 20:7, Matthew 18:19-20).

To worship God

Every time Christians meet on a Sunday, they implicitly declare the resurrection of the Lord. It is a day to fellowship and worship in celebration of the resurrection of Jesus. It is a platform to praise God, worship Him and testify about the goodness of God (Acts 20:7, Psalm 2:22).

---

[37] John Bechtle. *Why should Christians go to church? How important is it?* Available on line at http://www.christiananswers.net/q-acb/acb-t009.html

[38] Lang, G *The Churches of God: Their constitution, governance, discipline and ministry.* Paternoster Press. London. 1959

To grow spiritually

Going to church is not a waste of time but rather an essential part of a person's spiritual life and growth[39]. In the church service, the Christian has the opportunity of being taught the word of God, grow spiritually and experience God's joy (1Peter 2:2, Psalm 16:11). A new Christian who isolates himself/herself runs the risk of misinterpreting the scriptures.

For Corporate prayer

Christians are involved in spiritual warfare (Ephesians 6:12, 2 Corinthians 10:4). When Christians pray together, there is a corporate anointing present as Jesus is there with them. Whatever they ask in Jesus' name will be given to them as seen in the release of Peter from prison (Matthew 18:19, Acts 12:1-19). In unity, the church's power is multiplied (Leviticus 26:8). The church being together in unity is able to take its rightful place and destroy the works of the devil.

For accountability

---

[39] Deyoung ,K and Kluck, T. *Why we love the church: in the praise of institutions and organized religion*. Moody publishers 2009

Church membership provides an avenue for accountability as church leaders watch over the church members. Regular contact with other believers helps to motivate one another for good works (Hebrews 13:17-18). A Christian who answers only to himself may easily live in sin (1 Corinthians 5:1). Jesus says that if a brother sins he should be called to order (Matthew 18:15). This can only happen when a Christian is accountable to a local church.

To help one another

The church members are one body in Christ. When the Church comes together, the Holy Spirit is able to manifest with a variety of gifts (1 Corinthians 12, Ephesians 6:11-12). The gifts are to be used for church members to help one another (1 Peter 4:10). The love of Christ is made manifest when Christians love one another and use their gifts to edify each other [40](John 13:34, James 5:16). The gathering together the local church shows an acknowledgement of Christ's head of the church[41] (Colossians 1:13). Without the meeting of members of an institution, there is a risk of misrepresentation of the head of the organisation.

---

[40] Thomas, C *Life in the Body of Christ.* Founders Press 2009
[41] Wolston, W *The Church: What is it?* Bible Truth Publishers 1982

When the Church comes together, Jesus takes His place as the head and directs the affairs of the church (Matthew 18:19). In order to experience the presence of God that draws men to Christ, it is important that that church fellowship occurs. The church coming together with Christ as the head provides an avenue for the church to decree the will of God on earth and manifest the wisdom/glory of God (Ephesians 3:10-11, 1 John 3:8).

The church is not isolated from the head of the church. Jesus Christ and His body the Church are one. One cannot love one and hate the other (1 John 4:20). The love of God is manifested through the love of the church. Going to church is being obedient to the Head of the Church and is rewarded with the joy of making heaven and supporting one another.

References/ Bibliography

1   Bechtle, J. *Why should Christians go to church? How important is it?*   Available on line at http://www.christiananswers.net/q-acb/acb-t009.html . accessed on January 2011

2   Brown, L *The Life of the Church.* Broadman Press. *1987*

3   Grudem, W *"Systematic Theology"* .Intervarsity Press 1994

4   Lang, G *The Churches of God: Their constitution, governance, discipline and ministry.* Paternoster Press. London. 1959

5   Luehrmann, M *Lecture notes Church doctrine.* Faith Mission Bible Institute Edinburgh 2009

6   Harris, J *Stop Dating The Church: Fall in love with the family of God,* Moltnoma Publishers 2004

7   Wolston, W The Church: What is it

Chapter 6
The Awesomeness of Scripture

The authority of Scripture

The word authority is derived from the Latin word 'auctoritas'. It denotes the power or right to act in a designated way. The Word of God gives us the power to act in the ways of righteousness (Psalm 119:105). The Psalmist asks how a man can keep his way pure. It is through the reading of the Word of God (Psalm 119:1).

The authority of scripture conveys the Will of God for man to follow. We are not to be led by human intellect, philosophies or traditions of men. We are to be led by the authoritative Word of God. The Word of God is central to the establishment and growth of the Church.

Evidence for the authoritative nature of Scripture

The Bible scriptures are an inspiration for good works on earth. The scriptures have inspired men like Peter who were once fearful to preach the Word with power and authority (Acts 4:13). Conversely, the authority of Scripture is based in the inspirational character of scripture (2 Timothy 3:15). As Peter contends, no scripture is a matter of human intellect. Instead holy men spoke as they were moved by the Holy Ghost (2 Peter 1:21).

The importance of the authority of scripture

It is important to see the Word of God as authoritative as it contains the basis for the salvation of men. In a world, where moralistic traditions are vying to push away the relevance of the Word, it is important that Christians continue to affirm their belief in the absolute authority of the Word of God. There are not many ways to God. There is only one way of Salvation to God. That way is through Jesus Christ (John 3:16, John 14:6). In order words, the authority of the Scriptures is important because it demonstrates how man's soul can be converted to commune with God. The Word of God is essential for the development of sound doctrines that edify and are profitable unto good works (2 Timothy 3:15-17). As Brian Edwards affirms, the Word of God is flawless[42]. The Word of God contains the voice of God to lead us in our walk with God (Psalm 119:105)[43]. The Word is also important as it provides the absolute standard for all of human concerns[44].

It is important to see the Bible as the authoritative Word of God. A refusal to accept this fact will mean that men live their lives based on other philosophies with the Word of God just added as an appendage. The Bible is to be believed above all the research findings of men (Luke 16:31). The Bible is not to be a little attachment placed on the Christian walk. Due to its authority, the Bible is meant to be central in the Christian's walk with God. Christians need to study the Word of God to be approved in ministry (2 Timothy 2:15). It is to be treasured (Psalm 119:4). As Christians study and meditate on the glass of the Word of God,

---

[42] Edwards, B *Nothing but the truth.* Evangelical Press 2007

[43] Sheehan R Sheehan, R *The Word of Truth.* Evangelical Press 1998

[44] John Brand *Lecture notes on doctrine of scripture.* Faith Mission Bible College

they are transformed from one level of glory to another
(2 Corinthians 3:18, James 1:21, Romans 12:1).

The inspiration of Scripture

It is important to understand the inspiration of
scripture. When holy men wrote the scriptures, they
were inspired by the Spirit of God. It is always
important to note the inspiration of a piece of work.
The inspiration determines the direction of a particular
piece work. When we know that God inspired the
writing of the Bible, we can be confident that we are
following God's will and not that of man. Man's will is
flawed. In contrast God's Will as contained in His word
is flawless.

What does the inspiration of Scripture of Scripture mean?

The original greek word for inspiration is
theopneustos which combines 'theos' (God) and
'pnein' (to breathe)[45]. Paul asserts that the whole of
Scripture comes through divine inspiration. It is hence
profitable for teaching, preaching and formulation of

---

[45] Brand, J Lecture notes on doctrine of scripture. Faith Mission Bible
College 2010.

doctrines (2 Timohty 3:16-17). This is corroborated by Peter in 2 Peter 1:19-21. Holy men spoke from God as they were moved by the Holy Spirit. However, the Words still bear the marks of the cultures, experiences and predilections of the men who wrote them. Words that touch the mind may motivate, but they don't inspire.

It is only Words that touch the heart or spirit that can inspire. This is also confirmed in Job 32:8. Job says that it is a spirit that is in man and the '*inspiration of the Amighty*' gives them understanding. This suggests that inspiration has to do with the spirit of man and not just the mental intellect. This suggests that there is an impartation of the Spirit to give understanding when the Holy Scriptures are read. As Brian Edward affirms, the Scriptures originate from God breathing into man. Some of the prophets who God used to write the Scriptures heard from God. However, others saw visions and wrote as they were led by the Spirit[46]. The inspiration from the Word of God gives man understanding, wisdom and guidance on how to live on earth.

---

[46] Edwards, B *Nothing but the truth.* Evangelical Press 2007

The importance of the inspiration of Scripture of scripture

The divine authority of God's Word is based on its divine inspiration.[47] Without the divine inspiration, the Bible would lack the authority to influence the lives of men. Without the Holy Ghost inspiration, the Bible would just be another philosophical book with no power. However, because it is inspired by God, the Bible is able to transform the lives of men and win willing souls to Jesus Christ's salvation. The divine inspiration of the Word of God, gives it the power and authority to guide and direct the affairs of man.

It is important to see the Bible as inspired by God in order for us to obey it. The people who God used to write the Word of God were not robots. However, they allowed themselves to be enveloped in the Spirit of God, who moved them to speak and write His words. Based on the divine inspiration of the Word of God, Christians can confidently follow the dictates, preaching, teaching and doctrines that emanate from the Bible as they are written under God's divine Will and Providence.

---

[47] Brand, J Lecture notes on doctrine of scripture. Faith Mission Bible College 2010.

The sufficiency of Scripture

The Word of God is sufficient in itself to answer all the questions or challenges on man on earth. Nothing needs to be added to the Word for it to work. Notwithstanding, as the Bible proclaims, even nature itself speaks of the wonders of God (Psalm 19:1-4). As Wayne Grudem and John Brand argue, all scientific discoveries do is showcase the Hand of God in upholding all of creation in an orderly manner[48][49]. The Word is however the final authority on God that can convert the human soul (Psalm 19:7).

What does the sufficiency of Scripture of Scripture mean?

The sufficiency of Scriptures denotes the fact that Scripture is more than enough to settle all the affairs of men. In the time of fear, there are scriptures to help. In the time when peace or healing is needed, there is a scripture to settle every controversy. There is no need to add the philosophy of men to the scripture. The scripture is more than enough. Consequently, the

---

[48] Grudem, W *Systematic Theology* Leicester: IVP 1994
[49] Brand, J *Lecture notes on doctrine of scripture*. Faith Mission Bible College 2010

reformation declaration of 'sola scriptura' which means scripture alone is still relevant in our day and age[50][51]. The scripture is more than enough to teach us all things that relate with salvation and walking according to the will of God.

The importance of the sufficiency of Scripture of scripture

It is important to understand the sufficiency of God's word so that we do not add other things to the Word, to make it work. As Paul contends, the Word of God is sufficient in equipping the minister of God to do the work of the ministry (2 Timothy 3:16). Even with the advancement of technology and cultural changes, the Bible is still relevant in either implicitly or explicitly guiding the affairs of man.

Although there is some controversy among Bible scholars about prophecies and inspired publications that have been produced after the canonisation of Scripture, we need to rely on the Word of God for ultimate direction. There are additional Holy Ghost

---

[50] Sheehan, R *The Word of Truth*. Evangelical Press 1998

[51] Brand, J *Lecture notes on doctrine of scripture*. Faith Mission Bible College 2010

inspired works that can and do edify the Church. Notwithstanding, the Bible should be the final authority to settle all spiritual controversies and the not additional works or prophecies.

Contained in the Word of God is everything that the Christian and Minister of God needs for the edification of the Church. One of the names of God is El Shaddai. This means the God that is all sufficient. God is more than enough. In like manner, His Word is more than enough. If a Christian needs healing, deliverance or salvation the Word of God is able to do this (Psalm 107:20).

In the time of need, the Word of God is more than enough (Joshua 1:8, Psalm 1:3) An understanding of the sufficiency of the Word should prompt the Christian to take out time daily to study and meditate on it. No modern revelation can supersede the authority in the Word of God.

The clarity of Scripture

What does clarity of Scripture mean?

Clarity of scripture denotes the way in which spiritual things of God are propounded in scripture plainly so that both the learned and the unlearned are able to understand the meaning and apply the lessons of the Word of God. Issues that are central to the Christian faith are proposed explicitly. Examples include Jesus Christ dying on the cross of Calvary for man's redemption, the need for man to be born again to be saved and the divine inspiration of scripture (John 3:16, 2 Timothy 3:16).

Notwithstanding, there are deep mysteries in the Word of God that only the Holy Ghost can explain and reveal to the person who takes time to study the Word of God (1 Corinthians 2:7-9, Isaiah 64:4). We need the Assistance of the Holy Spirit for the Scriptures to become clear (John 14:26).

The importance of the clarity of scripture

The clarity of the Scriptures is important so that Christians read the Scriptures for themselves. The Scriptures can be understood by anyone who is a Christian and applies himself/herself to the Word under the tutelage of the Holy Spirit. Understanding of the scriptures is not under the control of church leaders or traditional church structures. It is important for Christians to also check the Word to see if what is preached is actually Biblical[52].

Despite Paul's laudable credentials, the Berean Christians in Acts 17:10-12 did not take what Paul taught at face value. They still went back to examine the Scriptures so see if what Paul was preaching was true. Contemporary Christians need to do the same today. Even though there is a place for being fed with the Word on Sundays, Christians need to grow by personally studying the Bibles themselves.

---

[52] Sheehan, R *The Word of Truth.* Evangelical Press 1998

The central tenets of the Bible are clear. However, some of the mysteries need unveiling by the Holy Spirit to be made clear. This may explain why the scribes and Pharisees in Jesus days did not understand the scriptures even though they were experts of the Law (Mark 12:24). However, with careful study and reliance on the Holy Spirit, the literate Christian should be able to clearly understand the Word of God. As Mark Thompson suggests, the Word of God is sufficiently unambiguous in the main for any well-intentioned person with Christian faith to interpret with relative adequacy[53].

An understanding of the clear nature of the Bible should inspire Christians to take time to study their Bibles, instead of waiting to be 'spoon fed' during Church services. Christians need to grow from the level of drinking the milk of the Word in sermons to eating strong meat of the Word through careful study of the Bible (1 Corinthians 3:2, 1 Peter 2:2, Hebrews 5:14).

---

[53] Brand, J *Lecture notes on doctrine of scripture*. Faith Mission Bible College. 2010.

The infallibility of Scripture

What does the infallibility of Scripture mean?

The Word of God is infallible. According to the Chicago statement on Bible inerrancy, 'Infallible' signifies the quality of neither misleading nor being misled and so safeguards in categorical terms the truth that Holy Scripture is a sure, safe and reliable rule and guide in all matters[54]. This suggests that the Word of God does not mislead.

The Word of God is reliable and hence profitable for direction. The Scriptures are in essence God's words. God has lifted His Word above all His names. God's Words are infallible. During Prophetic writings, there are references to the Words being the Words of God with statements such as 'Thus says the LORD' (Isaiah 5:3-6). Even in the New Testament, the Words of the Old Testament were regarded by the Jews are the Word of God (Acts 4:25, Acts 28:25)[55]. The infallibility of the

---

[54] Edwards, B *Nothing but the truth.* Evangelical Press 2007

[55] Brand, J Lecture notes on doctrine of Scriptures. Faith Mission Bible College. 2010.

Scriptures is a consequence of its inerrancy (that is being without error). Conversely, because the Word of God is infallible, it is also without error.

The importance of the infallibility of scripture

The infallibility of Scripture is very important to the Christian race. If the Scriptures are fallible then our faith would be in vain. This is because the words would have been the words of men rather than that of God. However, the Scriptures came into being as holy men spoke and wrote as they were moved by the Holy Spirit (2 Peter 1:19-21). The Scriptures are in essence God's words. Consequently, the Scriptures are infallible. Despite the onslaught from rationalists and controversial arguments from scientists, the Bible still stands strong as an accurate Record of history. It also provides guidance on how to live on earth. Our evaluation of the Word of God also determines our relationship with God.

All Scripture is inspired by God (2 Timothy 3:16). God is perfect and will not inspire something that is imperfect or fallible. An understanding of this relationship allows us to Worship God in the beauty of holiness. God and His Word are One (John 1:1-2). Since

God is perfect, the Words that He inspires are infallible (Psalm 119:140). Conversely, because God's Word is perfect and infallible, God is Holy and Perfect as He has exalted His Word above All His Name (Psalm 138:2).

The infallibility of the Scriptures is vital to the Christian faith. The gospel stories and paths of salvation propounded in the scriptures are not the result of wishful thinking of the writers of the Word of God. They are not philosophical opinions of men. They contain the commands of God. An understanding of this, allows the foundation of the Christian's faith to stand secure in the Word of God.

Jesus confirms that the person who hears His words and does them can be likened to a building that is founded on a sure, rocky foundation (Matthew 7:24). If we do not believe that the Word of God is infallible, our preaching will be without power or authority. An understanding of the infallibility will encase preaching/teachings with confidence and divine authority.

The inerrancy of Scripture

What does inerrancy of scripture mean?

According to the Chicago Statement on Bible Inerrancy, 'inerrant' denotes the quality of being free from all falsehood or mistake and so safeguards the truth that Holy Scripture is entirely true and trustworthy in all its assertions[56]. The inerrancy of Scripture denotes the fact that the Scriptures are without error. There is no mistake in the Word of God. There may be areas that superficially appear to contradict each other. However, when examined through the Lens of the Holy Ghost, they agree with each other. Even translations that contain marks or signatures of men who do the inspired interpretation are divinely guided to be without error.

The importance of the inerrancy of Scripture

The inerrancy of Scripture is important. If we believe that the Scripture is with error, then we will attempt to use other sources of information to supplement the

---

[56] Edwards, B *Nothing but the truth.* Evangelical Press 2007

Scriptures. However, the Scriptures are sufficient to assist us in living godly lives according to the will of God. If the Bible is with error, then it would not be the Word of God. God is perfect and everything that emanates from God is perfect (James 1:17). Since we know that all scripture is inspired by God through the orchestration of the Holy Ghost, we can be confident that the Scriptures are without error (2 Timothy 3:16). Down to the smallest detail, the Word of God is accurate and reliable[57]. Bible antagonists have gone to great lengths to demonstrate supposed errors in the Bible. However, as Robert Sheehan argues, there are no errors in the Bible[58]. There are problems which are easily resolved through Truths in a linked Scripture.

The Word of God is without error. With this knowledge, the Christian can be confident that his/her salvation is secure as it is based on the undefiled Word of God; that is pure and perfect (Psalm 119:140). The Scriptures reflect the glory of God. Hence, an understanding that God's word is without error affects our attitude to God. If we believer that His Word is

---

[57] Brand, J *Lecture notes on doctrine of scripture*. Faith Mission Bible College 2010.
[58] Sheehan, R *The Word of Truth*. Evangelical Press 1998

perfect and without error, then we will have an equally high regard for the God who inspired the Scriptures in the first place.

When we accept the Bible's inerrancy, we will have no grouse in accepting the accounts of creation or other miracles in the Bible. A non-acceptance of the inerrancy of the Word of God may lead to a person trying to supplement the Word with the philosophies of men. If we do not believe in the inerrancy of the Word of God, we may be tempted to agree with untrue philosophies and theories of men (For example, the theory of evolution). The Word of God is true. The Word of God is tried by fire. The Scriptures are more perfect than Gold (Psalm 12:6, Psalm 19:10, Psalm 119:140). The Scriptures are infallible and inerrant. Through the Scriptures, a Christian may find salvation, peace and deliverance.

Bibliography/References

1   Brand. J. Lecture notes on doctrine of scripture. Faith Mission Bible College. 2010
2   Edwards, B *Nothing but the truth*. Evangelical Press 2007
3   Fee, G and Stuart, D *How to read the Bible for all its worth*. Scripture Union. 1993

4 Goldsworthy, Graeme – 'Gospel And Kingdom' in Goldsworthy's 'The Goldsworthy Trilogy – Paternoster (2000)

5 Roberts, Vaughan – 'God's Big Picture' – IVP (2002)

6 Sheehan, R *The Word of Truth*. Evangelical Press 1998

Chapter 7
The canonization of Scripture

Canonization is the process whereby divinely authorized scripture are collated into a collection of books that is useful for teaching, preaching and edification. The word canon comes from the Greek word, 'Kanon'[59]. It means a reed. A reed was used as a measuring rod. The canon of scripture denotes the rule or standard by which teachings from preachers, pastors and other ministers can be judged. Any teaching that contradicts the canon of scripture is to be rejected. The Holy Ghost orchestrated the writing and canonization of the Scriptures. The scriptures were written over about 1500 years through about 40 human writers[60]. Although there are historical and archaeological evidence to support the authenticity ofthe scripture, we believe the Scriptures are from God through faith.

---

[59] John Brand *Lecture notes on doctrine of scripture*. Faith Mission Bible College
[60] Edwards, B *Nothing but the truth*. Evangelical Press 2007

Stages of canonization

There are about three stages that occurred for canonisation to take place. These include inspiration by God, recognition by men of God and collection and preservation by the people of God. The Holy Spirit moved or inspired men to write (1 Timothy 3:16). The Hand of God was moving throughout the process of inspiration, authorisation and canonisation of scripture as the Holy Ghost orchestrated the whole process.

Inspiration

As Peter contends, no scripture is a matter of human intellect. Instead holy men spoke as they were moved by the Holy Ghost (2 Peter 1:21). The Old Testament is traditionally divided by the Jews into the Law, the Prophets and the Writings. With the Old Testament, the scriptures were written by inspired Prophets such as Moses. Moses is believed to have written the first five books of the Bible (the Pentateuch or the Law), while other holy Prophets wrote the rest of the Old Testament.

The writings in the New Testament were written by Apostles who were inspired by God. Strict exceptions include the book of Hebrews, James and Jude. James and Jude are believed to have been brothers of Jesus, while the Hebrew writer may have had close associations with Paul as the style of writing of the Hebrew writer closely resembles that of Paul. Historical evidence suggests that Mark and Luke are believed to have had authorisation by the Apostles Peter and Paul respectively[61][62].

Holy Recognition of the Scriptures

Jesus implicitly alludes to the authenticity and authority of the Scriptures of the Old Testament as we know it by referring to Abel (Genesis) and Zechariah (Zechariah) in Matthew 23:35-36. Jesus recognises the authority of the Old Testament Scriptures in John 10:32-34.

---

[61] Brand, J Lecture notes on doctrine of Scripture Faith Mission Bible College 2010

[62] Scroggie, W *A guide to the Gospels*. Pickering and Inglis Ltd 1973

In Luke 24:44-45, Jesus reveals that the Scriptures of the Old Testament testify of Him. 10% of Jesus words include about 150 quotations from the Old Testament[63]. Jesus argues strongly that the Scriptures cannot be broken (John 10:35, Matthew 5:8). In John 5:39, Jesus commands that the Scriptures should be studied for in them we think and have eternal life. Authority of scriptures is not limited to the Old Testament.

The New Testament is also recognised as being part of Scripture. Paul's epistles are equated to the Scriptures by Peter in 2 Peter 3:15-16. From 1 Corinthians 14:37 we can deduce that Paul writes the commandments of God. However, he appears to contradict himself in 1 Corinthians 7:14 when he says he is now speaking from personal opinion. Notwithstanding, even is personal opinion under the guidance of the Holy Ghost is still stamped with

Authority by God as His Holy Word. God also stamps His authority on the epistles of Paul when Paul says *'which things we speak not in words which man's wisdom*

---

[63] Sheehan, R *The Word of Truth.* Evangelical Press 1998

teacheth, but which the Holy Ghost teacheth' (2 Corinthians 2:13).

Paul validates the authenticity of Luke's gospel for canonisation by referring to Luke 10:7 in 1 Timothy 5:18. Similarly, John argues that Apostolic teachings are from God (1 John 4:1-6).

Collection of the scriptures by people of God

The collection of the Old Testament took place over a prolonged period of time. The collection of books was done organically or spontaneously under the guidance of God. Moses expected the law to be canonised (Exodus 24:4-7). Prophets were commanded by God to write down the Word in books that were later to be canonised (Jeremiah 26:18, Hebrews 2:2). The concurrence or agreement of different parts of Scripture with each other is evidenced by numerous cross references (for example, Jeremiah 26:18 and Micah 3:12 or Daniel 9:2, Zechariah 7:5 and Jeremiah 25:11-12).

The collated Holy Books were placed in the temple of God by the children of God. From Deuteronomy 31:24-27, we can understand that the book of the Law was kept by the Ark of the Covenant. In 2nd Kings 22:8, Hilkiah the High Priest finds the book of the Law in the House of the LORD. The Words of the book are read to King Josiah in 2nd Kings 22:11. The Jewish council of Jamnia in 70AD officially formalised the canonisation of the books of the Old Testament. A copy of the Dead Sea scroll containing the Old Testament intact was found in 1947[64].

The Apostles who wrote letters to one church expected their letters to be circulated to in all brethren other churches (1 Thessalonians 5:27, Colossians 4:16). The epistles and gospels that make up the New Testament were collected by the early Christians. They were used for exhortation and edification. They bore the inspiration of God and are part of Scripture. Again, they were collected organically by the church and not necessarily by a Church council.

As Scroggie reveals, the Four Gospels were universally accepted in the Catholic Church as trustworthy records of Jesus' life. Around the end of the 2nd century the Gospels were revered as sacred books by dispersed community of Christians. New Testament scrolls containing the Gospels and some

---

[64]Edwards, B *Nothing but the truth.* Evangelical Press 2007

epistles were found in 1740 (the Muratorian canon)[65]. Canonisation was undertaken in response to persecution, to combat heretic teachings and in reaction to the church growing world-wide.

Why we should trust the canon of scripture

For the books to be regarded as Scripture, the books had to have had Prophetic or Apostolic authorship. The books needed to come with the authority of God. They had to be authentic, dynamic, and received, organically collected, read and accepted by Children of God as the Word of God.

Based on these criteria, we can be confident that the Scriptures are the Words of God. Notwithstanding, our trust in the scripture is based on internal validation in the Word of God (the scripture itself) and simple faith in God's Word. Jesus says that blessed are those who do not see the evidences but still believe (John 20:29). This faith is ignited when we hear the Word of God (Romans 10:17).

---

[65] Edwards, B *Nothing but the truth.* Evangelical Press 2007

Praying God's Word

Living the Christian life is a fantastic adventure. The key is meditating on the Word of God. The Word of God also has to be prayed. As John Wesley *says "Prayer is where the action is"*. I know that you can do this. Greater is He that is in you than he that is in the world. You ae more than a conqueror in Jesus' name. I pray that the deep Truths in God's Word enriches your life and take you to your place of peace and breakthrough in Jesus' name.

Bibliography/References

1 Brand. J. Lecture notes on doctrine of scripture. Faith Mission Bible College. 2010

2 Edwards, B *Nothing but the truth*. Evangelical Press 2007

3 Fee, G and Stuart, D *How to read the Bible for all its worth*. Scripture Union. 1993

4 Goldsworthy, G *The Goldsworthy Trilogy..* Paternoster 2000

5 Roberts, Vaughan *God's Big Picture* IVP 2002

6 Scroggie, W A guide to the Gospels. Pickering and Inglis Ltd 1973

7 Sheehan, R *The Word of Truth*. Evangelical Press 1998

<u>To Give your life to Christ</u>

Pray this prayer with me.

Father LORD, I thank you for sending your Son Jesus Christ to die on the Cross of Calvary. I believe that He died and rose again on the third day for my justification. I repent of all my sins. LORD Jesus come into my heart as my LORD and Saviour. I am born again. Greater is He that is in me than he that is in the world. Fill me with your Holy Spirit and help me to walk in holiness and righteousness. By faith, I acknowledge the covering and protection of the precious blood of Jesus over myself, my family and all my possessions. Thank you, Lord, for saving me in the name of Jesus. Amen.

ABOUT THE AUTHOR

Dr Kingsley Oturu is a Medical Doctor, a graduate of University of Sokoto, Nigeria with a special calling to teach the Word of God. A British-Nigerian, he hails originally from Ariam Usaka, Ikwuano LGA, Abia State, Nigeria.

He has a diploma in expository preaching from Faith Mission Bible College, Edinburgh and a PhD in international Health from Queen Margaret University, Edinburgh, Scotland UK.

He is from a Christian home and gave His life to Christ while at King's College Lagos in 1989. He is a Public Health Specialist and works with a variety of educational and health institutions in the UK and globally. He has a passion for helping the underprivileged and is a serial social entrepreneur setting up international charities (such as the Prevention and Control of HIV/AIDS Foundation, the African Scottish Development Organization-www.asdoonline.org.uk and the Holy Ghost Chapel-www.holyghostchapel.org). He is author of scientific articles and Christian publications.

Combining recent medical/scientific research, research experience and expositions from the Bible, he gives apply theological underpinnings of the gospel in your life to practically living the Christian life. God bless you in Jesus' name.